WOULD YOU RATHER?

RATHER?

BACHELORETTE
PARTY GAME

DIRTY EDITION

D1450399

Would You Rather?
Game Rules

1. First, congratulations on getting married!
2. One player is asked a question. The bride-to-be should go first.
3. The questions can be asked in any order or the reader can go front to back.
4. Once she has answered the question, the rest of the players also answer the same question.
5. If the majority of the group agrees with the player, she gets a point.
6. Use the score sheets in the back of the book to keep track of points.
7. Remember, there are no winners or losers!
8. Or simply ditch the game, pour some booze, and have fun asking each other questions!

Would you rather give up masturbating for a year or sex for a year?

Would you rather your partner be able to orgasm without ejaculating or get hard again right after ejaculating?

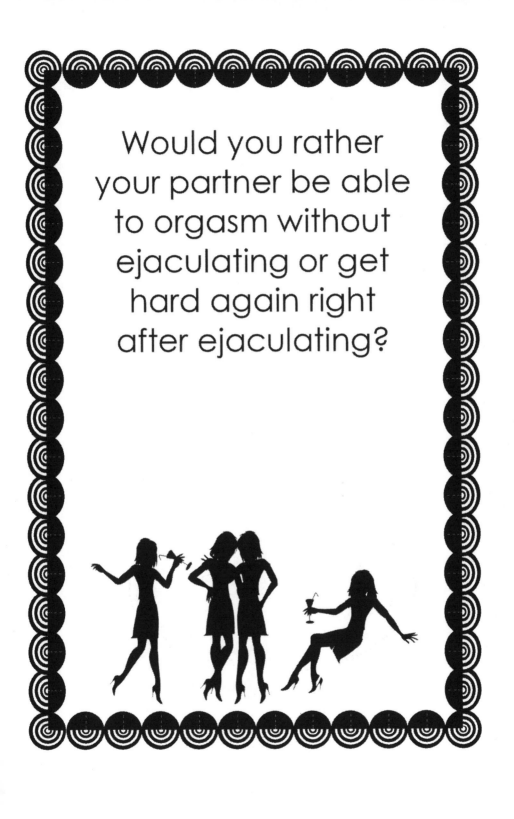

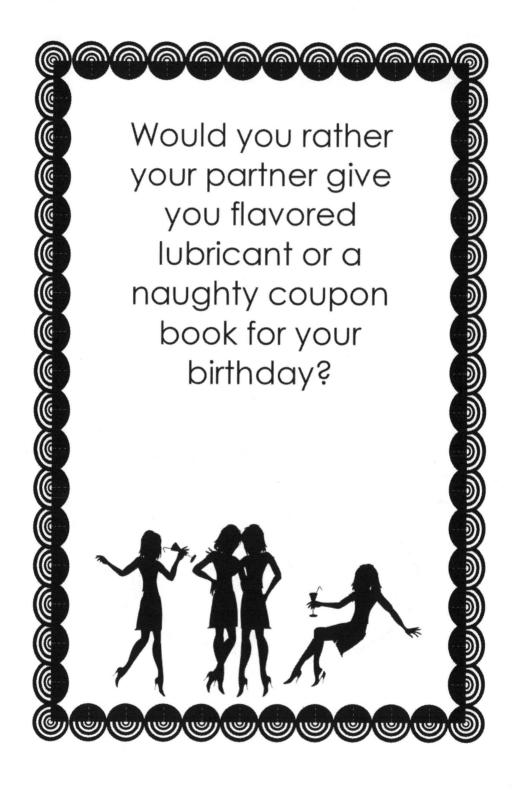

Would you rather your partner give you flavored lubricant or a naughty coupon book for your birthday?

Would you rather give up sex for ten years to stop animal cruelty or have sex every morning to feed the children?

Would you rather
have sex in a walk-in
cooler or a sauna?

Would you rather be told you are bad at giving oral or a bad kisser?

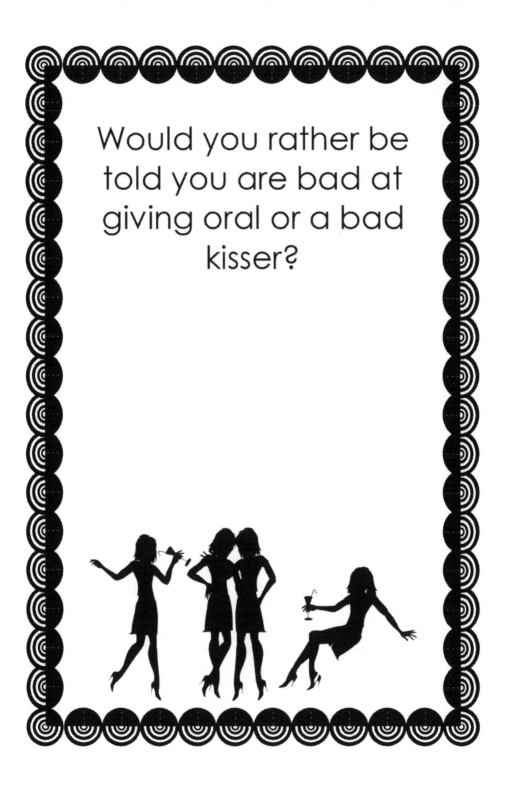

Would you rather use a stranger's toothbrush or use a stranger's anal beads?

Would you rather your partner's fetish be for him to have sex dressed as a clown or dressed as a nun?

Would you rather he sneezed in your face during sex or didn't stop talking during sex?

Would you rather give your partner oral while he's driving or get fingered on a Ferris wheel?

Would you rather have a social media post that showed your ass or your nipple?

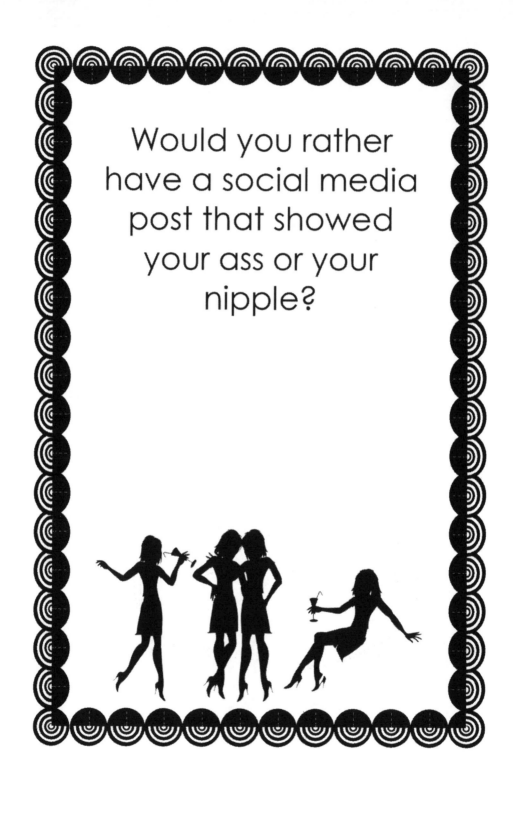

Would you rather have sex with Justin Bieber or go down on George Clooney?

Would you rather have your partner always laugh during sex or cry during sex?

Would you rather have sex in a public park or in your parent's bed?

Would you rather have sex with one of your friend's husband or a hot porn star?

Would you rather
have sex in a hotel
bed with
questionable sheets
or a public
bathroom stall?

Would you rather your partner have a small penis that never went soft or a big penis that sometimes didn't work?

Would you rather get your butt fingered or finger his butt?

Would you rather have casual sex when you haven't waxed or haven't showered?

Would you rather know the name of every person your partner slept with or get a free pass to sleep with one of your exes?

Would you rather your partner be a sex addict or he stop being interested in sex after a year?

Would you rather
have sex with a
second cousin or
have your period in
front of a hot
coworker?

Would you rather read about an orgy or watch an orgy?

Would you rather
your partner didn't
find you sexually
attractive anymore
or only loved you for
your looks?

Would you rather have unprotected sex with your ex or unprotected sex with the UPS man?

Would you rather watch hot gay guys in thongs on a beach or kids and middle-aged men with dad bods?

Would you rather grant your partner's request for a golden shower or his request for you to sniff his underwear?

Would you rather suck your partner's toe or lick his armpit?

Would you rather accidentally send a nude picture of yourself to your father or to your boss?

Would you rather have a third person watch or participate?

Would you rather have sex with someone who breathes heavily or yelps?

Would you rather have sex with someone with a small circumcised penis or a large uncircumcised penis?

Would you rather
your partner walked
around calling his
penis
"The Jackhammer" or
"The Bone Ranger"?

Would you rather your partner always wants to be dominated in bed or have a partner who likes to bite?

Would you rather have your partner see your dirtiest underwear or your number two in the toilet?

Would you rather have sex in a bubble bath or the shower?

Would you rather go skinny dipping with your immediate family or with your partner's immediate family?

Would you rather your partner always orgasmed after one minute or one hour?

Would you rather be tied up in bed or blindfolded in bed?

Would you rather your partner suffers from coprophilia (arousal to feces) or was still a virgin?

Would you rather your partner be totally hairless or have extreme body hair like a gorilla?

Would you rather during sex he yelled out an ex's name or his mother's name?

Would you rather
your partner had
man boobs or an
extra toe?

Would you rather always be really horny at two in the morning or two in the afternoon?

Would you rather have a partner who didn't make a noise when orgasming or who only wanted to do it missionary style?

Would you rather
have your hair
pulled or your
bottom spanked?

Would you rather your partner accidentally ejaculated on your mouth or in your ear?

Would you rather accidentally fart while having sex with a new boyfriend or during a parent-teacher conference?

Would you rather sleep with a guy who had the face of Ryan Reynolds and the body of Clint Eastwood or the face of Woody Allen and the body of Adam Levine?

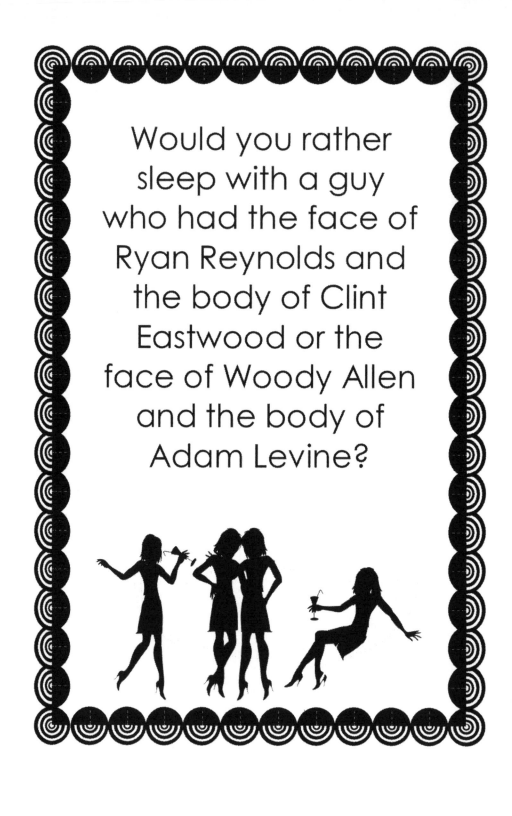

Would you rather bring a dildo into the bedroom or whipped cream?

Would you rather
watch girl-on-girl
action or guy-on-
guy action to get in
the mood?

Would you rather your partner had uncurable back acne or a three-inch erect penis?

Would you rather be on top or on bottom all the time if you could choose only one position?

Would you rather hear your partner say during sex, "I'm going soft" or "Did you do this with your ex?"

Would you rather he said your juices were like runny snot during oral sex or that he always referred to sex as "intercourse"?

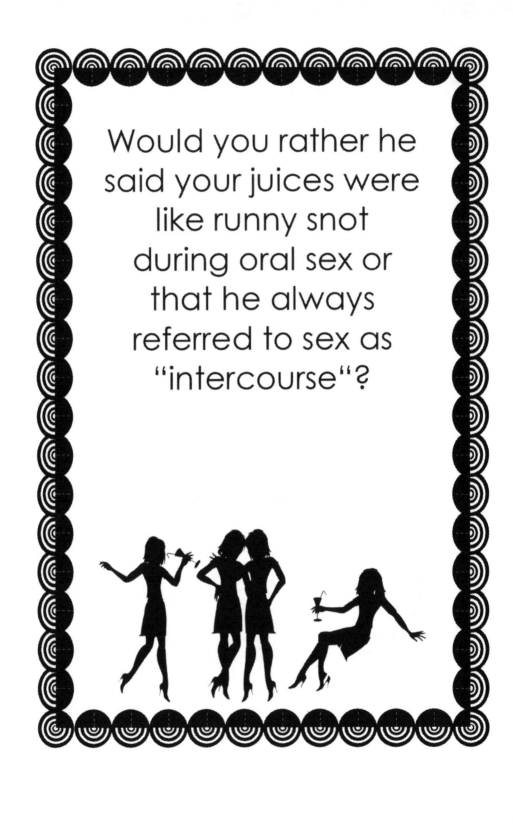

Would you rather be excellent with excellent with finances or excellent in bed?

Would you rather find out your partner slept with 200 women or experimented with men college?

Would you rather your partner do a sexy strip dance for you or you be able to do a strip dance at a club with no consequences?

Would you rather he always shoots a little in your hair or always shoots all over the bedding?

Would you rather your partner seduced you by singing and dancing to "Let's Get It On" or stripping to his tighty whities to "That Old Time Rock N' Roll"?

Would you rather find someone else's used tampon in your bathroom or a used condom you don't recognize?

Would you rather change something on your partner's face or something on your partner's body?

Would you rather he checked his phone while you were having sex or he acted annoyed it was taking you so long to orgasm?

Would you rather your partner like to dress in women's clothes or like to take it up the butt?

Would you rather allow your partner to sleep with someone for $1000 or know that your husband donated to a sperm bank?

Would you rather have drunken sex or spontaneous daytime sex?

Would you rather have a sex toy get lost up your butt and need to go to the emergency room or contract an STD?

Would you rather
your partner call you
"Mommy" or
"Baby Girl" in the
bedroom?

Would you rather your parents walk in on you having sex or you walk in on your parents having sex?

Would you rather have group sex with three strangers or three of your exes?

Would you rather have sex with someone three feet taller than you or a foot shorter than you?

Would you rather
your partner refuse
to engage in public
displays of affection
or refuse to go down
on you?

Would you rather accidentally throw up during sex or start having diarrhea?

Would you rather start accidentally watching your parents' sex tape or have them accidentally start watching yours?

Would you rather tell a small lie to spare your partner's feelings or be completely honest and have great make-up sex but now he doesn't trust you?

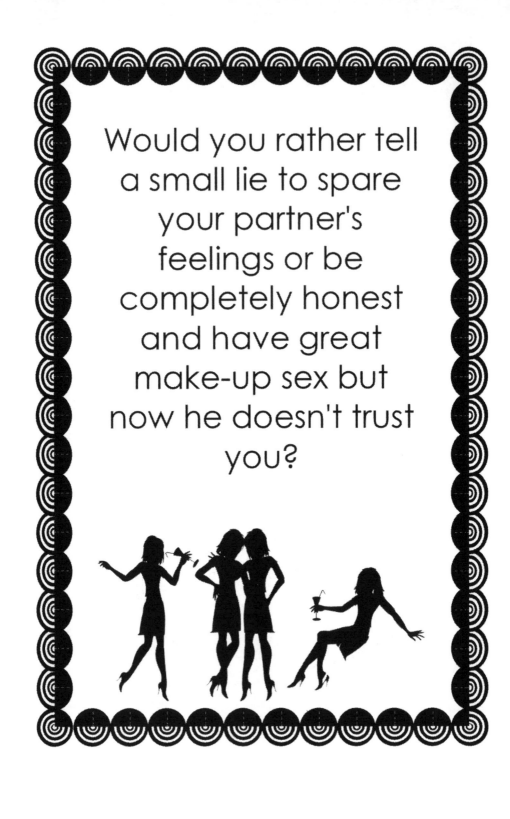

Would you rather have sex with your partner's father or one of his brothers if no one would ever find out?

Would you rather everyone know your internet search history or your partner's internet search history?

Would you rather your partner's skin be very flaky or slightly slimy?

Would you rather be a marketing manager for a sex doll company or Summer's Eve?

Would you rather let your last Uber driver or your last pizza delivery guy finger you?

Would you rather your partner's fantasy be to have sex in a human-sized kitty litter box or for you both to be dressed up like cats?

Would you rather have oral sex with a woman or allow your partner to have a one-night stand?

Would you rather
cuddle every night
or be woken up
every morning with
oral sex?

Would you rather have foreplay for an hour or sex for 10 minutes?

Would you rather have sex with other people in the house and the lights on or with all the windows open and the lights off?

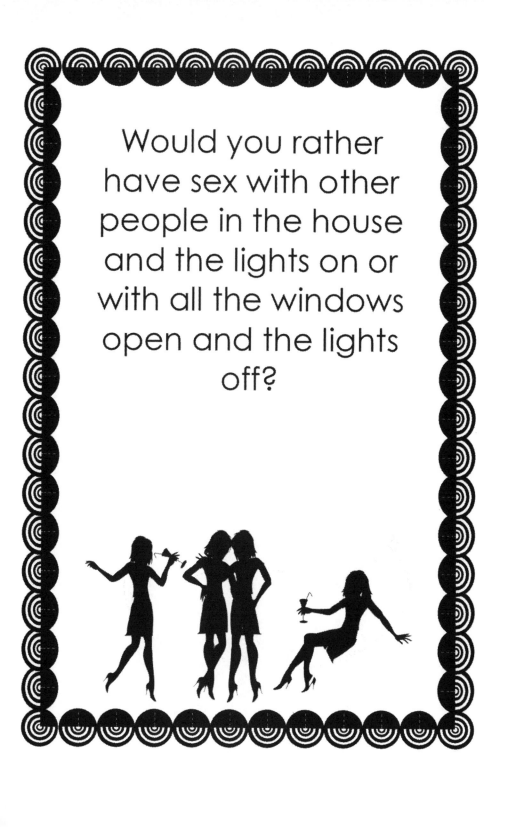

Would you rather
have sex on a
pinball machine or
your boss's desk?

Would you rather
suffer through
carpet burn on your
knees or a big
purple hickey on
your neck?

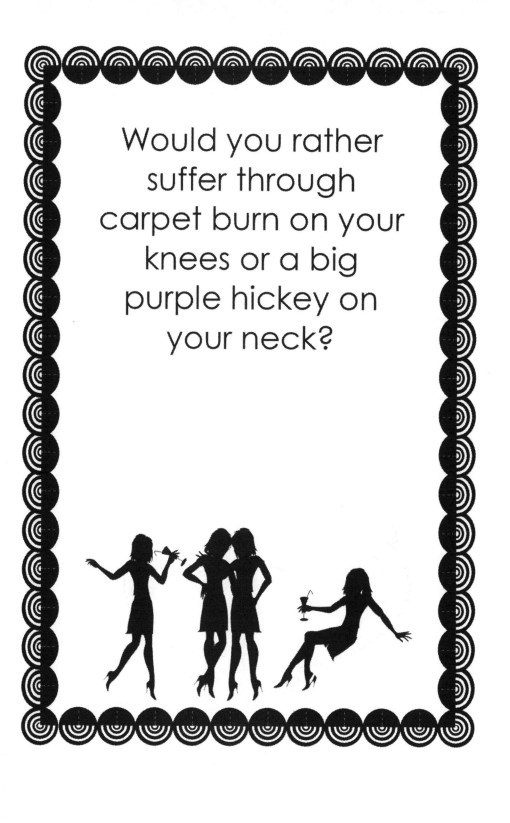

Would you rather your partner have a really great butt or really nice eyes?

Would you rather
your partner had a
high squeaky voice
or was terrible in
bed?

Would you rather have casual sex with the repairman or your next-door neighbor?

Would you rather dress up as a sexy nurse or he dresses up as a sexy doctor?

Would you rather sleep with an eighteen-year-old and afterwards have to use his dirty shower and ratty towel or with a 68-year old in a hotel suite with champagne and a city view?

Would you rather
your partner have
an exceptionally
long penis or an
exceptionally fat
one?

Would you rather
have all your sexual
fantasies come true
or keep some in your
head?

Would you rather give up having cramps or give up good sex?

Would you rather wear edible underwear or use candle wax to turn on your partner?

Would you rather hear your partner say during sex, "What should I do next?" or "You remind me of my mom."

Would you rather
your partner be
totally lazy during sex
or have him
constantly grabbing
your head to show
you where to put
your mouth?

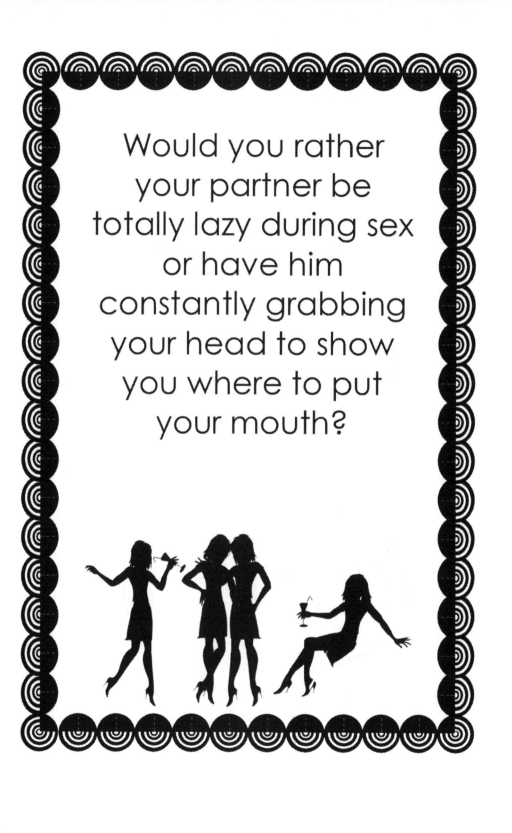

Would you rather your partner slept with his boss for a pay increase or slept with your best friend so she could get pregnant?

Would you rather have a porn video accidentally start playing loudly on your phone in the grocery checkout line or see your homemade sex video with your face blurred out on a porn site?

SCORE SHEETS

Name	Points

Name	Points

Name	Points